How to Open a Mobile Coffee Business

Bring Your Morning Wake-up Beverage to On-The-Go Customers

Calantha Pemberton

© **Copyright 2024 - All rights reserved**.

The content contained within this book may not be reproduced, duplicated or transmitted without direct written permission from the author or the publisher.

Under no circumstances will any blame or legal responsibility be held against the publisher, or author, for any damages, reparation, or monetary loss due to the information contained within this book, either directly or indirectly.

Legal Notice:

This book is copyright protected. It is only for personal use. You cannot amend, distribute, sell, use, quote or paraphrase any part, or the content within this book, without the consent of the author or publisher.

Disclaimer Notice:

Please note the information contained within this document is for educational and entertainment purposes only. All effort has been executed to present accurate, up to date, reliable, complete information. No warranties of any kind are declared or implied. Readers acknowledge that the author is not engaging in the rendering of legal, financial, medical or professional advice. The content within this book has been derived from various sources.

Please consult a licensed professional before attempting any techniques outlined in this book.

By reading this document, the reader agrees that under no circumstances is the author responsible for any losses, direct or indirect, that are incurred as a result of the use of information contained within this document, including, but not limited to, errors, omissions, or inaccuracies.

Table of Contents

Introduction..5

Chapter 1: Why a Traditional Coffee Shop is Not a Good Idea for Most..................................6

Chapter 2: How to Get Your Coffee Business Brewing..10

Chapter 3: Cart or Truck? And What You'll Need to Buy to Start.......................................22

Chapter 4: How to Sell More Coffee in Person...27

Chapter 5: Pricing Structure and Ironing Out Details..40

Chapter 6: How to Get More Gigs from Online Marketing...50

Chapter 7: Expanding Your Cart Business Beyond One Cart...61

Conclusion..65

Introduction

Coffee is not only something that tastes delicious, but it's a staple for many people's morning routine. Our lives are so hectic and busy that we oftentimes find ourselves needing coffee in order to function. Let's face the facts though, making coffee from a $20 coffee maker at home just isn't as good compared to getting coffee at a coffee shop. This is why people are often willing to spend upwards of $5-$6 for coffee. Those are definitely some high-profit margins. What if though, you were able to create this same high-quality coffee experience for people, but you brought the coffee to them? They didn't have to go out of their way on their commute or it was just there for whatever event you were doing? That's what makes a mobile coffee business so unique. All of a sudden, it's not just about the coffee anymore, it's an experience wrapped around an everyday beverage. And throughout this book, I want to share with you how you can make this dream a reality, so let's get to it!

Chapter 1: Why a Traditional Coffee Shop is Not a Good Idea for Most

I'm sure that you're a big coffee lover, so naturally it makes sense to want to work with coffee in some capacity. You might have a dream of opening your own brick-and-mortar store one day, and if so, that's great. In the beginning, though, I do believe that starting out with something mobile is going to make more sense for you initially. This isn't to say that as time goes on you can't transition into a brick-and-mortar because you certainly can. Here are a few reasons why I would wait on a physical location when you're first starting out:

Too Much Money Upfront

The first and most obvious reason why you should wait for a brick-and-mortar is because it's going to cost an insane amount to get things off the ground. You're going to have a deposit and then you're immediately spending thousands on your lease. This is money that could be poured into promoting your business. It can be a scary thing to know that you have a lease to pay for every month when you're just trying to get things going. That's a lot of pressure for anyone. Instead, you can start to build your brand and keep things cheaper to start. This way if you decide this business isn't for you, then it's no big deal in the long run.

Locked into a Lease

Another difficult aspect of signing a lease is getting the right space. If you've never operated a physical store before or had to scope out a location for one, then there are quite a few things that you have to think about. Some things you might not even think about until it's too late. A big one is the amount of space you'll need. This of course is hard to predict. You don't want to get too much space and overpay, so oftentimes people will get a space that ends up being too small. They need to move and expand, but it becomes more of a challenge once you're locked into those lease terms. You could also move in and then discover that your location isn't as good as you thought, there isn't enough parking, the layout isn't that good, and many other things. With a lack of experience, this is a lot to handle and you don't want to get stuck with something that's hard to deal with.

A Better Alternative

Luckily though, there is a better way to start out and that's by going mobile. When you go mobile, you can either do that via a truck or a cart. If your budget is a bit more tight, you can start out with a cart and then transition to a truck, and now you'll have the best of both worlds. There are scenarios where you'd want a truck and cases where you would want to have a cart. A cart does give you a lot of options to serve people at a cheaper starting price, so keep that in mind. With lower start-up costs and not getting locked into a lease, you can spend that extra time and money on networking and marketing your business. This means you'll be able to put your first dollar of profit into your pocket sooner rather than later. Additionally, as I mentioned in the intro, you're bringing coffee to people, which is a different twist from how most experience getting coffee. They're already rushing and they're late for work, now they have to wait in a long line to get their coffee. With you, let's say you set up an agreement with a business office. You'd come in with your cart, stay for an hour or two as everyone is arriving, serve them coffee, and then leave. Now the employees of that company get to skip the line, walk straight into work, and get their coffee. How cool is that? This is just one of the many possibilities of how you can use your coffee cart. Think about bridal showers, baby showers, engagement parties, family reunions, town events, at church, the list goes on and on for where you can serve coffee to people, so needless to say there is a lot of opportunity when it comes to a mobile coffee business.

Chapter 2: How to Get Your Coffee Business Brewing

Before we get to the fun stuff of getting customers and making some money, there are some things you're going to need to do and look into first to get your business up and running. Sure this isn't fun, but it's all part of the process.

Business Name, Formation, EIN, Bank Account, Domain Name, Etc.

One of the first steps to starting a business is establishing your business. This may or may not be the first step that you want to take. You want to do your research first regarding the laws and regulations surrounding starting a food business, more specifically a coffee business in your area. Either way, this is something you're going to have to take care of sooner than later. The first step in the process is coming up with a name. Entrepreneurs will go back and forth on how much time you should spend picking out a name. I think that you should think carefully about this as it is your brand. A name influences how someone thinks and feels about your business, so it is important to think about. The key is to not go with something solely on how you feel about the name. Instead, give your friends and family a list of names and have them choose the one they like the most. See if their responses line up with the name that you like the most. Yes, this is your business, but your business isn't about you, it's about the customers. What you don't want to happen is to pick a name that ends up being confusing for customers or doesn't land with them. You might be thinking one thing, but because it's your business, you might be blind to how your potential name could come across as unclear. Other people though will be thinking with an outside perspective just like your customers. So if there's a name on your list you really want, ask people why they chose a different name, or you can ask them why they chose the name that they did. No matter what, taking some time and getting feedback on a potential name is a good idea for your business.

Business Formation

Once you've come up with a name, it's now time to go ahead and register your business. You have some different options when it comes to the type of entity that you want to create. I recommend consulting with a professional to help you decide which entity is the right choice for you. Essentially, you can have a corporation, limited liability company (LLC), or a sole proprietorship. In most cases for a single member forming a business like this, an LLC is going to be the most viable option. It will help to give you some protection unlike a sole proprietorship, and it won't be too much like a corporation likely would be in this case. To file your business with the state you reside in, you can consult with a business attorney to help you through this process, or you can use a website such as Legal Zoom to help you out. The cost to file your company with the state will vary depending on where you live. For example, in Texas, it costs $300 to file your LLC with the state as of the time of writing. In California, you have to pay an $800 annual franchise tax. Some states are considerably favorable to file an LLC in, such as Nebraska or Wyoming. Something you definitely shouldn't do is try to register for a Nebraska LLC while you live in another state. These states offer these benefits as an incentive to try and get businesses to move to their state, so register to form your business in the state you reside in.

EIN

If you decide to go the sole proprietorship route, then you don't have to get an EIN, which stands for employer identification number.

Instead, you can use your personal social security number for tax purposes. If you register as an LLC, then you will get an EIN number, which is used to help identify your business for tax purposes.

Bank Account

Regardless of what entity you choose, you need to open a separate business bank account so that you can keep all of your business finances separate from your personal finances. This helps to keep things clean and organized, and it makes things much easier for tax and bookkeeping purposes. There are plenty of great online options that you can explore that don't involve you ever having to step foot in a bank, which is nice.

Domain Name and Hosting

In the world of the internet, it's weird for a business to not have a website. So you're going to want to secure your domain name using a website such as Go Daddy or Name Cheap. However, having a domain name isn't enough, you need a website host that will ensure your website is live 24/7 so it can be seen at any time. A couple of good options for this are Host Gator or Blue Host. Your domain name is going to be cheaper than hosting and how much your hosting will cost you will all depend on which package you choose, but typically you can get your website hosting for $15-$20 per month.

Insurance

Since you're dealing with something that people are consuming, it's important to get some business insurance to help protect you in the event something does go wrong. Look into getting a food liability insurance policy, which can help against claims such as someone getting sick from consuming your coffee, and a general liability policy as well, which can help provide coverage if someone is hurt because of your cart or something along those lines. Working with an insurance broker can help provide you with the coverage options that are right for your business.

Design Your Website

One seemingly daunting task you need to take care of is designing your website. Just because you have a host for your website, doesn't mean that your website is going to look good. The idea of designing your own website can sound intimidating, but you don't have to pay hundreds or thousands for someone else to do this for you. You can use beginner-friendly templates with drag-and-drop features to make it easy to create a design that you like. There are plenty of options for this. The following are some I recommend:

- Shopify
- WordPress
- Wix
- Squarespace

If there are certain technical features you want your website to have, you may have to hire someone. But if you're not sure, I highly recommend you watch some tutorials online as the process really isn't as bad as it seems. Do your research on some of the options I've listed here and see what you like best. Here are some of the things you'll want to be sure to include on your website:

Contact Form

One of the biggest mistakes a website can make is making it difficult for a visitor to get their questions answered. So if you don't have a contact form, you're going to be missing out on potential sales. Someone likely will have a question you've never thought of, so you don't include it on an FAQ. Now the customer just has to assume an answer to their question because your website doesn't have a way to contact you. This is a nightmare scenario that you want to avoid at all costs. The contact form itself can be simple enough where all someone needs to fill out is their name, email address, and then the question they need answered.

Order Form

Another crucial mistake is not having an order form on your website. Sure, most people will likely want to have some form of communication with you before they buy, but some people will gain all of the info they need from your website and act on it. They don't need to talk to you or anything like that. So as long as you're able to get the details you need from your sign-up page, then you'll be good to go. Doing this will make for an easy way to get sales without you having to even think about it.

Place to Collect Email Addresses

Some people are going to like what you're doing, but they're not going to be quite ready to be a customer just yet. That's totally okay and realistic. What you want to do though is collect some type of information from them so you can stay in regular contact. This way you can start the process of having someone who's a cold lead and start warming them up over time. They'll start to know you and your business better and the likelihood of a sale happening will increase. You could just put a simple sign-up form on your website for an email address. If you do this, don't expect much of any results to come from it. Instead, you have to do something to incentivize someone to want to part ways with their email address in a sense. There's so much spam out there nowadays that the last thing people want is another email. But if your reward is enticing enough, people will give you their email, and if your regular emails are good enough, people will continue to stick around on your list, which is exactly what you want. So what type of incentive should you provide? Well, typically this would be something like a free ebook. So if you were selling beauty products, your incentive might be something like a free ebook where you go over your makeup routine. For this business, you could try and come up with an idea for a free ebook. However, something that would be good to give away would be a coupon for 10% off of their order when they book your cart.

About Me

This part of your website is less about the business and more about who you are. Think of this like your bio section, except you don't want to make it sound boring. Talk about your background, your passions, and what it was that drove you to want to start this business in the first place. You want to captivate people with your story here. Maybe you went to college and studied finance. After working in the corporate world for a few years, you realize you were left unfulfilled and that you wanted to do something different. During your time in finance, you became addicted to caffeine to help you push through the long hours you were working. So you figured hey, now that you're drinking coffee on a regular basis anyways, why not make a business out of it? That's just an example, but you have a story and people want to know about it. Your story takes you from some faceless business to an actual person that others can connect with. That is a huge turning point and it makes a difference when it comes to sales and your brand.

Process for How You Make Your Coffee

Something other coffee businesses might not think of is sharing their process for how they make their coffee. This is something that can allow you to showcase what makes your coffee so special. You're not just providing a service where you make an average cup of joe from some cheap coffee maker. No, your coffee is far better than that, so you might as well let your customers know what your coffee is all about so they can feel confident in what they're signing up for.

What Makes You Different?

In the same section where you're talking about how you make your coffee, you can talk about what makes your coffee company unique. The fact that you are a mobile coffee company is very different, and it's something that depending on where you're operating from no one else might be doing. So you'll definitely want a place on your site where you talk about how your company works from an operational standpoint. Explain how you bring the cart to them and how you can make custom drink orders or premade drinks for people to grab and go after an event. Since this concept is new, many of your website visitors may not be aware of how your service works, so you'll want to make sure you talk about it.

Payment System

You're going to need a way to collect payment from people. There are plenty of different ways that you can do this, so there's no need to worry. The first thing you need to think about are the types of payment you'll accept. Typically this is going to be card or cash, but you could accept other forms of payment such as PayPal, Venmo, Apple Pay, and others. It's important to think about this ahead of time because you don't want to be scrambling to try and accept a certain type of payment if you're dealing with a long line. If you're dealing with a client that's paying you to be at their engagement party and serve the guests coffee for free, then I recommend keeping it simple and only accepting some type of digital payment to keep things simple and have a history of the transaction. If you're at an event where you're selling coffee to individuals, then this is where you'll want to accept as many forms of payment as you can because you don't want to miss out on a sale because you don't accept a certain form of payment. So how do you accept credit and debit cards in person?

Well, you have a few options here. The first is to use a card reader from Square. The other option you can use is a card reader from Shopify. For taking care of payments directly from your website, you can use something called Stripe or you can use Shopify's payment system. If you set up your website using Shopify, then you can also use their point-of-sale system to help you handle collecting payments.

Accounting Software

Last but certainly not least you're going to need a way to keep track of your expenses and income, which you can hire a bookkeeper for if you don't want to keep track of things yourself. If you're looking for an option to be able to do this yourself, then Quickbooks and Wave Accounting are some good options to look into.

Chapter 3: Cart or Truck? And What You'll Need to Buy to Start

When you're starting this business, one of the biggest decisions you need to make is how you want to provide your coffee. Do you want to operate out of a truck or from a cart? Both scenarios will come with their own pros and cons, so bear that in mind. In this chapter, I want to discuss the differences between a cart and a truck, and what kind of supplies you'll need to get this thing going. Bear in mind that if you are struggling to choose between a truck or a cart, just know that your decision isn't permanent. You can always start with a cart and move to a truck later on. If you start with a truck, it will be harder to move away from that expense, but it can still be done and you can solely operate a cart or utilize both.

What Advantages Does a Truck Offer You?

When you're using a truck to operate from, all of your materials and supplies are permanently set up. All you have to do is drive to where you're going and then start making coffee. With a cart, you're going to have more to set up and take down every time you go somewhere. You also have more space to work with and can serve a lot more people from a truck. You could even bring on some extra help in a truck to serve even more people. The more people you're serving, the more you're able to make, so the ceiling for your earning potential is higher with a truck. Granted, there are some advantages that a cart will offer you over a truck.

What Positives Does a Coffee Cart Give You?

One thing about a truck is that it is going to cost more to get going than a cart will. A cart will also give the ability to move around easier. So if a place wants you to operate indoors, you'll be able to do that. So given the cheaper cost and the wide range of customers you can serve, it makes sense to start with a cart as I mentioned earlier. If you know you want a truck, you can start with that right out the gate. If you're a little unsure, then just start with a cart and set aside your profits to put towards a potential truck one day. Later on, you may still want to operate a truck or you might want to just stick with a cart.

What Regulations Will You Be Subjected To?

Given that you are in the food and beverage industry, there are going to be some rules and regulations that your business is going to be subjected to. The tricky part is that the regulations for your coffee business will differ from someone else's based solely on the state you're residing in. So be sure to contact the health department in your area to learn more about the regulations in your area. They'll be able to help guide you to get your coffee business ready to go. With that being said there are some common things you'll likely have to look into such as a three-compartment sink with a splash guard between each section, a fresh water and grey water tank, hot water heater, hand washing sink, commercial grade fridge, and being subjected to annual or semi-annual inspections.

What Supplies Will You Need?

Regardless of if you're looking to start a coffee cart or truck, here are some of the supplies you're going to need to buy to get things going:

- Coffee Maker
- Coffee Tamper Maker

- Espresso Maker
- Microfiber Cloths
- Tamper Station
- Espresso Shot Measuring Cup
- Coffee Grinder
- Water Filtration System
- Coffee Handle
- Milk Frothing Jug
- Pitchers
- Spoons
- Cooler for Ice Storage
- Trash Can
- Cleaning Supplies

There are some other items you'll want to think about as well. For instance, if you're working from a truck you're going to need electricity to operate your machines. So the easiest option here is likely going to be using a generator, but solar panels are a potential option as well. With a cart, you'll want to ensure you're within reach of an outlet and you can use an extension cord if needed. One cart-specific item that could be worth looking into is a small trailer. This will allow you to easily transport your cart without having to break it down and then reassemble it every time you need to transport it. You'll want to make sure that the trailer you get won't be too much for your current vehicle to handle and that the trailer has a ramp to make for an easy on and off every time.

Chapter 4: How to Sell More Coffee in Person

This part of the book is going to be very important for your success. We're going to be talking about how can you land more clients with in-person methods. This is very important as this is one of the ways in which you'll be able to get your business off of the ground. Maybe you've heard people talk about how you just have to get started and customers will come naturally. Sure this does sound good in theory, but it doesn't work in the real world. You have to make yourself known in order for people to become customers. Simply starting a coffee cart business won't bring you customers automatically. You're going to have to be willing to work to earn your customers, but luckily after this chapter, you'll know what you need to do to make that a reality.

Why Cold Outreach is Your Best Bet for Your Coffee Business

When you need to generate revenue for your business, there is no shortage of options at your disposal. The best way to grow your business though is going to be with cold outreach. The idea of this may sound scary, but you're not going to have to spend any money like you would with ads. And most ads need to be tweaked along the way to fully optimize them for a good return on investment. Not only that, but what if your message isn't being seen by the people who have the highest likelihood of being interested? By approaching your target customers directly, you ensure that you're speaking to people who have the highest chance of caring about what you do. Sure, going up and talking to people you don't know is intimidating, so I can understand if you feel hesitant about this concept. What I will tell you though is that you have nothing to fear. The majority of the time when you're talking to business owners or individuals, people aren't going to be rude to you. They may not be interested in what you're presenting, but they're likely not going to be mean about it. Think about yourself when someone stops by your residence to pitch something to you. Are you rude about it or polite? Even if someone is rude to you, they can't hurt you, but a yes will help you for the better, so keep that in mind before you write this idea off. There isn't a cheaper or more effective way to instantly create cash flow for your new business than this, and it will get easier to do as you continue to do it. So how do you grow your mobile coffee business with cold outreach?

It Starts With Who

If you just try and go out into the world and start talking to people, things aren't going to go well for you. You need to take some time and plan things out first before you do anything else. You need to know who you want to talk to and what you want to say. If you talk to bakery owners, that's great that you're trying to expand your business, but you're wasting your time because the average bakery owner isn't going to need what you have to offer. If you do talk to the right person, but you don't know what to say, you're going to stumble over your words, you won't sound confident, and people will be hesitant with what you're offering. You only get one shot at a first impression so you have to make the most of each place that you approach. If you botch it on your first try, then chances are slim that you're going to be able to talk to them again later on and have anything come from it. The first piece of the puzzle we need to tackle here is going to be who we want to talk to. Think about the types of businesses and people that you want to put your brand in front of. It really can be anything as there's a whole host of companies and individuals that could be interested in your services. The following are some examples:

Any Business Office

One of the great parts of running a mobile coffee business is that there is no limit to the opportunity. Seriously, any business office could use your service. Essentially what you'll do is come in the morning, set up, serve coffee to the employees as they come in, and then leave. You can set this up to where the employees buy their own coffee from you or the company pays per hour for you to be there and you make the orders for the employees. With this, you can approach business after business and before you know it, you can create a full schedule for yourself. Most businesses are going to be operating from 9-5, but there are plenty of other shifts that exist as well. There are mid-shifts where people might come in at 10 am or noon or a second shift where people would come in at 2 or 3, for example. With this being the case, you can stagger things across multiple businesses. So you might serve coffee to the morning workers at one company and then go do a different company and serve people who are coming in for a mid-shift. There are no limits when it comes to this, so you should be hitting up every business you can to try and fill up your schedule. It doesn't matter if it's large or small businesses either. Sure you can make more from a larger business, but small businesses can be easier to get a hold of the decision maker, which can increase the chances of getting a deal done. Don't assume either that a small business won't be able to afford you. When you do that, you are rejecting yourself. You have to let them reject you because you won't know if they'll be interested or if it's out of their budget until you talk to them.

Cities

It's a good idea to get in contact with city offices as well. This will help you to start to form connections with the right people so that way when city events do come up, you'll be someone who comes to mind. You can serve coffee at events for a certain period of time, and a lot of city-held events will occur on Saturdays, which can act as a good supplement to supplying coffee for businesses' employees during the week.

Anyone in the Event or Wedding Industry

Establishing connections with the right people in the right industries is a huge part of your success. One such type of industry you should focus on are people who are in the wedding industry. Not just weddings and people who are getting married, but the event industry in general. The reason being is that it's an easy sell. An easy way to enhance an event is to have coffee. And what about for weddings? Well, it's the same type of thing where having a coffee cart or truck at a wedding will add to the celebration. It doesn't matter when the wedding is either because people don't drink coffee solely in the mornings. On top of that, some people will have their wedding on a Sunday because venues are cheaper on Sundays than on Saturdays. Having a coffee cart for a wedding on a Sunday makes perfect sense. It's not just the wedding though. There are bachelorette parties, engagement parties, bridal showers, rehearsals, and so much more. There are plenty of opportunities for you to be able to show up over the course of someone's engagement. So in this case you'll want to hit up vendors that are in the wedding industry, and individuals as well. Building a relationship with vendors is key because they can give you leads or you can work with them directly. So in the case of a wedding photographer, for example, they may get a client who's getting married and suggest your services. In exchange, if you know of someone who's in need of a wedding photographer, then you can suggest them. If it's something like a wedding venue, then you can partner with them to be a part of the services that they can suggest to couples who sign up to use their venue. So there's plenty of opportunity to be had regardless of which direction you go in.

What Gets Measured Gets Managed

You have an idea of the types of businesses and people that you'd like to reach out to but that's not enough. If you start to approach businesses and do not see any success, it will be easy to write this idea off. What if the problem was that you actually didn't approach as many businesses as you first thought? If you don't measure the activity you're doing, then you have no idea if you should be upset or not over your lack of success. Take dieting for example. Someone may be frustrated that they're not losing any weight when it seems like they're barely eating anything at all. However, if calories aren't being tracked, then the reality could be that the person is eating more calories than they realize. Once calories start getting tracked, then the realization kicks in of being surprised just how many calories certain foods contain. It's no different here. You have to talk to a lot of people to get to a yes. And in order to be successful you have to measure your data. This way you'll know what's wrong so that you can fix it. So for instance, if you've talked to 250 different businesses and haven't had one of them book you, then you know you need to change up your approach. Knowing that you've talked to 250 people versus feeling like you've talked to a lot of people is very different. By tracking, you'll know if your success rate is about where it should be. So how do you go about tracking your data to know if your approach needs to be tweaked or not? Well, step number 1 is going to be creating a spreadsheet. The first thing you're going to want to do is list out the names of companies on the first column. These are going to be the companies that you're going to want to talk to. Then in the next column, you can have a check box to signal if you've talked to them initially or not. The column to the right of that can be a checkbox to indicate if they've signed up or not, and lastly, you can have a couple of columns for the date when you initially talked to them, and a column for when you followed up. By creating a simple spreadsheet like this, you can now easily know how many companies you're talking to on any given day. You'll know the date you talked to them so you can wait an appropriate length of time before you follow up. Most importantly, you'll know your success rate. You'll know if something is off with your approach. So what would be considered a good success rate with something like this? Well, you're really looking for about 1% of the people you talk to to sign up with you. So if you talk to 100 different companies, you'd want to get at least one sign-up. This of course seems really low and that's because it is. These people that you're going to be talking to don't know who you are, and to be quite honest most are not going to be interested. That's just the way it is, you have to talk to a lot of people who aren't interested to get to the people who are interested. By tracking the data you'll know if you're seeing a 1% sign-up rate or not from your efforts. Without tracking, you'd have no idea if you've even approached 100 different establishments. So don't freak out panic or anything along those lines until you've talked to 100 different places and have seen no success. If that happens, then you need to start dissecting things to determine where you're missing the mark. It's not just about the words you're saying. It's body language and tonality as well. In fact, tonality and body language are more important than the words you're saying. Imagine if you had the perfect words to say, but you came in and said them without any conviction or without confidence. How successful do you think you would be? Obviously, you're not going to see much of any good results. So a good tip that you can follow is to practice in the mirror. Look at your body language and make sure that you're speaking with conviction. Practice over and over again so that way you're not stuttering over your words or anything like that. Don't worry though, I'm not going to leave you hanging when it comes to what you should say.

How Should You Talk to Different Companies?

There are a ton of different approaches and ways that you could talk to someone about your services. So if you don't like something, or you want to tweak something, you can always do that, test it, and see if it works. My recommendation is to keep things simple. People are busy and you don't want to take up too much of their time. More importantly, you don't want to take up more of your time. If your pitch is super long and they're not showing any initial interest, then you're wasting time that could be spent going to the next person. So I like to think of things like an elevator pitch where you're in an elevator with someone and you only have 30 seconds or less to pitch them on your services. If they're interested you go from there to get them to sign up. If not, you move to the next person. This is an idea of what I would say:

"Hey I'm Matthew with Matthew's Mobile Coffee Shop and I was wondering if people at this company drink coffee?

They respond yes.

"I figured who doesn't right? The reason why I'm talking to you today is because I was wondering if your company might be interested in my services. Essentially, I'll come in for an hour or two in the morning, serve coffee to people as they're coming into work, and then leave. Before I bore you with any more details that will make you need a coffee, does this sound like something you would be interested in?"

The goal with your pitch is that you need to keep it simple and make sure that it doesn't confuse people. The fact that you're a mobile coffee shop will intrigue people enough to make them want to hear what else you have to say. Hence why you want to start off with mentioning that you're a mobile coffee shop. From here, you want to explain what you do in a way that's simple for people to understand. You won't be able to cover small details like your menu in your initial pitch, and that's fine. You're trying to give enough info to gauge interest and then they can ask additional questions to help fill in some of the details. You also want to ask questions to help guide the conversation along. By asking if people drink coffee, you're subtly saying, "Hey everyone is in need of what I have to offer here." By asking if they're interested in the last portion, you're forcing them to give you a direct answer. If they sound hesitant, tell them you can set up a time to come in and give everyone some free coffee to try it out for themselves. This way you can let your product do the talking and seal the deal for you. One additional layer to this is who you're talking to. Normally, you're going to be talking to a receptionist or secretary. This isn't going to be a person who will make the decision to hire you or not. Most oftentimes, the receptionist isn't going to bother bringing up your business to their boss. However, that is the case with most businesses. In your case, it's more likely that they will because you're dealing with something that can directly impact them and improve their life. If they don't have to wait in line to get their coffee and now they can leave their home that much later, then that's a plus for them. If they're excited about the opportunity, then they'll mention it to the decision maker and this is where the chances of gaining a new client will dramatically increase. You see, it's different when a decision-maker is approached by someone they already know and trust, in this case it's the receptionist. If the receptionist approaches their boss enthusiastically about what you presented, then it's going to greatly increase your chances as opposed to you talking to the boss directly. This is good news because normally it's a hard fight to be able to talk to the person who can make the decision, and that's why these endeavors can fall flat on their face. With this unique business though, it plays to your advantage to talk to the receptionist.

Chapter 5: Pricing Structure and Ironing Out Details

When you do come across someone who's interested in your services, what do you charge them? Coming up with different price points can be a stressful process. If this is your first time running a business, it can be easy to sell yourself short. In fact this is what most beginners do. They don't feel confident in what they're offering or that someone would pay them good money for what they're doing. They end up working long hours, feeling underpaid, taken advantage of, and sometimes left wondering if it's all worth it. Having these feelings are the last thing that I want you to be dealing with in your mobile coffee shop. Pricing is something you'll want to carefully consider before you try to pitch your services. This chapter will help to guide you along the way and give you some suggestions to help ensure you feel good about your prices.

Know Your Numbers

The first piece of the pricing puzzle you must determine are your hard costs. You need to know how much it costs you to make a cup of coffee and you need to know how long it takes you to make a cup of coffee. Why does the length of time to make a coffee matter? It's a big deal because this will help to determine the number of customers you can serve. Here shortly, you'll learn about the different ways that you can charge for your service. If you're charging by the cup, for example, and you know that it takes on average 3 minutes to serve a customer from start to finish, then this means you can serve about 20 people per hour. By knowing this information, it can help you determine how much you want to charge per cup. You could take your price per cup and multiply it by 20 to determine if that's a maximum hourly rate that's worth your time. Of course, this would be your gross income. If you don't know how much it costs you to make a cup of coffee, then you won't be able to determine how much profit you can make from each cup that you sell.

Different Ways You Can Charge for Your Coffee

Something cool about a mobile coffee business is that you're not limited to one way of charging. You can charge differently based on what the scenario is or in some cases what the client needs. If you were selling a physical product, then you would be more limited and you'd typically only charge one rate for each product sold. This added layer of flexibility will help to ensure that you don't waste your time with any event that you do, regardless of how big or small it is. You'll simply adapt to ensure you're maximizing profit based on the size and type of location you're in.

Charge by the Hour

One of the simplest ways that you can charge is by the hour. In this scenario, whoever it is that is in need of your services will pay for your services and then you will serve coffee for a predetermined amount of time for free to anyone who comes to your stand. So for instance, this could be a church that pays for your cart to be at their establishment for 5 hours to cover both of their Sunday morning services. The church would pay you for 5 hours at your predetermined hourly rate, and then you would serve coffee to people for free during that timeframe. The nice thing about charging by the hour is that it doesn't matter how many people you serve, the money you make is still the same. You could serve 5 people over a 2-hour timeframe and it doesn't matter, the money you make is still the same. This is why charging by the hour makes a lot of sense if you think the event might be on the smaller side.

Even if it's not, you can simply adjust your hourly rate to accommodate having to serve more people. So what is a good hourly rate to give you an idea of what you could be charging? Well, something along the lines of $100 to $150 per hour is going to be a good range. This of course can seem like a lot because it's just coffee. But it's far more than that. You have to consider the gas it's going to take to get there, the cost of goods to produce your coffee, and the additional amount of time you're going to spend setting up and taking down everything. When you think about all of these things, it starts to become very clear as to why you'd need to charge in this realm to make things worth your while.

Charge by the Event

Instead of charging by the hour, you can charge for the entire event. So let's say someone wants you at their wedding and they want you there for the entirety of the wedding. You can charge a flat rate and be there for the duration of the wedding. The thing about charging in this type of manner is you have to ensure that you pad things a bit. You want to overestimate the amount of time you'll be at the event, and you'll want to consider how many people will be at the event. When charging by the event, it can be easy to sell yourself short. You won't want to feel like you're overcharging the customer, so you're very exact with how long you think you'll be there and how many people you'll be serving. So if your normal rate is $100 an hour and you think you'll be at a wedding for 5 hours, you don't want to charge $500. Instead, you're going to add on a bit from what you're initially thinking to help pad the numbers in case things go on for longer than you expected. It's not a bad idea to add on a couple of extra hours just in case. For this example, that would mean you'd charge $700 for the wedding rather than $500.

Charge by the Cup

The last way you can charge is by the cup. When it comes to changing by the cup, you can have each individual pay for their cup of coffee, or if the establishment you're serving at is paying you, then you can keep track of the coffees you make, calculate the total cost for all of the beverages sold, and then send an invoice after the event is done. So how much should you charge for a cup of coffee? Well on average somewhere in the realm of $5-$6 is going to be a good spot. Sure your coffee prices aren't going to be the cheapest, but that's not the point. You're trying to make things worth your while and make a profit. Nowadays people aren't going to bat an eye at paying that much for a coffee because that's what a lot of specialty places are charging anyways. When it comes to charging by the cup, it can be tricky. If the place is really busy, it can be more of a challenge to keep up with the number of drinks you've made. If the place isn't that busy, then you run the risk of not making enough money for it to be worth your time. Imagine if you sold coffee for $5 per cup and served 6 people over the course of an hour. This would equate to a gross amount of $30, so your profit would be less than that. If you charge the right amount at the right place, charging by the cup can work out for you. However, more than likely in the beginning you're going to be better off charging by the hour. This will ensure that you're generating guaranteed income for your business and that you don't accidentally sell yourself short.

Questions to Ask Before Landing a Client

Generating new business is going to be an exciting feeling for you. What isn't fun though is to be excited for a new client only to realize you're not able to get your cart up their steps or that there's not an electrical outlet nearby.

Some things can be a pain to deal with and others could cause you to not be able to complete the job. That's why there are some details you need to think about and ask before someone signs up to ensure everyone is on the same page.

Will a Ramp be Available?

The first thing you're going to need to ask is if a ramp will be available for you to be able to get your cart where it needs to go. Trying to get your cart up steps is not going to be practical and you run the risk of damaging something. This is a small detail that can instantly derail an event if you're not even able to get your cart to the spot it needs to be in.

Electrical Outlet

Some of the equipment you're going to be using is going to require the use of electricity so you'll want to ask where the closet outlet will be in location to your cart set up. If you're out of range, then you can always use an extension cord. The smaller the cord you can use the better as this will create less of a potential tripping hazard for people and whatever is plugged into the cord might come flying off with it! If you do have to use a long extension cord to reach an outlet, it's not a bad idea to invest in some cable ramps. It could be possible that you won't even have an outlet available for you to use if you're outdoors. Knowing this information ahead of time is crucial so that you can plan ahead accordingly by getting something like a portable power station.

Roughly How Many People Will You Be Serving?

A great question to ask before you go over pricing is to try and get a rough estimate for the number of people that will be at the event. This way you can help to plan accordingly for how you'd like to charge, such as by the hour or per cup, for example. This will also help you know how much prep time you'll need and if you'll want to keep a simple menu or not. If you're going to be serving a lot of people, then it doesn't make sense to have a long menu or a menu with complicated items. The more complex your certain drinks are, the longer it's going to take you to serve people, which means you'll be able to serve less people overall.

How Long Will I Have to Serve These People?

This is another question that's critical to ask, but it's something you likely wouldn't think about. Let's say you're in a situation where you're serving people after a church service is released or a conference speaker finishes and everyone is released for a break. You're suddenly going to go from serving no one to serving a bunch of people at once. If you're taking custom drink orders, then you're not going to be able to serve everyone. So if the break is 15 minutes before everyone needs to be back in their seats, then not everyone is going to have the chance to be served. If it's something like a business office where people will be trickling into work over the span of an hour or two, then this is no problem at all. By asking this question ahead of time, you can help to set the expectations. You could say, "Hey, if you need me to serve 175 people over the span of 15 minutes, I'm not going to be able to do that by taking custom orders. What I can do though is have the drinks pre-made so that way people can just grab and go." The person hiring you likely won't be thinking about the logistics side of things, which is why you need to think about these details and talk about them beforehand.

Date of the Event and Location

These may seem like trivial details in the grand scheme of things but it's important to nail down the date and location and stay updated with it. What you don't want to happen is a miscommunication where the date changed but nobody told you. Now on the day of, you're showing up to a place where no one is at. If this happens, you'll want to ensure that you're collecting a deposit so that way you're not wasting your time if a mistake is made.

Approximately How Long Will You Be There?

Another piece of the puzzle to help you best determine how you want to go about charging is to ask roughly how long you'll need to be there. This will help you figure out how much supplies you need to bring, if additional help would be needed, and of course, determining your price point.

Chapter 6: How to Get More Gigs from Online Marketing

Going around and trying to gain clients in person isn't the only type of marketing that you need to be focusing on. In fact, you need to mix it up with some online tactics too. With marketing online, you can help expand your reach to people who never would have known about you. Another plus to online marketing is that it's easier to do it anytime anywhere. When you're marketing in person, you're going to be bound to a location and it can only be done within certain timeframes. If you're approaching businesses, then you're going to have to do this during normal business hours. With online marketing, there are no boundaries and you can put as much time into that as you want. By combining online marketing methods with in-person, you can truly create a powerful force to create new customers for your business.

Search Engine Optimization

What if instead of you having to approach people, they came to you? Doesn't that sound like a nice change of pace? With search engine optimization (SEO), you can do just that. Every day people in your area are using online search engines to look up various things. You've done this as well. Maybe you've searched for a hair salon near me or fast food near me. When you do that, different businesses will pop up and you can do more research by looking at their website and their reviews. Well, you can set things up to where people will find your business this way too. What you'll need to do is set up a Google My Business account. This way, whenever someone searches for something like a mobile coffee shop, coffee shop, or coffee shop near me, your business will have the chance to show up. When it comes to competing for search terms like coffee shop, it's going to take a while for you to rank high in those results because there are going to be other established brick-and-mortar shops that you're competing against. More niche searches, such as mobile coffee shop, will be easier to compete for from the start, but it will still take time. This is why doing cold outreach where you're approaching people is still so important. The idea of people coming to you is how we'd all like for things to be ideally, but that doesn't happen when you're new and trying to get things off the ground. You need to be able to force the action and get new clients as quickly as possible. SEO is more of a long-term play that you want to invest in from the beginning because it will pay off for you. When it comes to making the most of SEO, there are some basic things you want to do. First, make sure you attach your website so that it's easy for people to see your business, go to your website, and then learn more about you. It's happened to me plenty of times where I wanted to go to a company's website from the business listing, but it wasn't connected so I just moved to the next company. You want all of your information to be easy to access so no one has trouble finding the info they need. If they get frustrated, they're going to go to someone else. The other major factor is going to be your Google reviews. When you're starting out, you're obviously not going to have any reviews, so again, people who do find you from an online search are going to be a bit skeptical. You're also not going to be able to build up your reviews until you start serving clients, so you have to get clients first to be able to start generating reviews. Again, are you starting to see why leaning on SEO from the start is going to have you waiting a while before you get your first customer? Instead, you have to force the action, get your first client, and then make sure you do your due diligence to get a review. Organic reviews online do happen, but they are very rare. The chances of someone leaving you a review on their own is going to be very small. Asking someone one time to leave you a review is going to increase your chances, but again it won't be likely. You have to follow up with someone again and again to try and get them to leave a review. So what's the optimal way to go about this? Whenever you're finishing up and getting ready to leave, thank the client again for letting you serve them. Then ask if they wouldn't mind leaving you a review as it would really help make other people aware of your business. The majority of people are going to say yes. However, you may not actually get a review. While people have good intentions, people don't want to do something that's inconvenient for them if there's no incentive for them to do so. I'm not saying you need to bribe people, what I'm saying is that you need to make it easy for people to leave you a review. If someone had never left a review online before, they're not going to spend a lot of time trying to figure it out. So it's up to you to make the process simple and straightforward, so minimal effort is required on their part. How do you manage to do that? What I recommend is that you create business cards and on the card is a QR code that your customers can scan that will take them straight to the page where they can leave a review for your business. This way everything is simple and easy on their part. You can even include some basic instructions on your business card for them to follow once they scan the code so there's no confusion. This is going to be step one. If you don't see the review after 24 hours, go ahead and contact them again asking if they could leave a review. You'll want to follow up in as many ways as you can. So if you have their phone number and email, send them a text and an email. We'll want to follow the same premise here of making things simple for them, so we'll want to include a link that will take them straight to the review page. If they don't get back to you or if they say they'll leave a review but haven't after 48 hours, then you'll want to follow up one more time. Yes, you might feel like you're being a bit annoying with how many times you're asking, but you have to ask multiple times to get things done sometimes. Your initial customers leaving reviews is critical for getting the ball rolling. If you take the proactive steps to make the process simple for them to leave a review, then you will have a much higher chance of getting a review to begin with so hopefully you won't have to follow up multiple times.

Content Creation

There will be some people who will be intrigued by the idea of what you're doing, but they may not be ready to be a customer yet. Over time though, you can help to warm them up and convert them into a customer. A great way to stay in regular contact with your ideal customers is to be on social media. People will give you a follow because of the type of business you're doing. It's unique and fun and people will want to be a part of that. By regularly creating new content, you can continually stay in front of your audience and help warm up people to the idea of using your service. How do you create content as a coffee business in a way that isn't repetitive and boring? Well, you just have to be creative. Play to your strengths in addition to doing the things that seem regular. Since you're a mobile coffee business, post about your cart or truck. Give a tour of your truck if that's how you're operating. Show people the ins and outs of your cart. Tell people about a new item that you're adding to your menu. If you can make latte art, that's a great idea as well. Any time you're going to a place to serve coffee, post about it. This helps to provide social proof and that you're staying busy. Post about what your favorite kind of coffee is or post a poll on your story asking people which kind of coffee they like better. There's a host of ideas and opportunities here as long as you're willing to think a little bit as to what you want to post.

Why Most Struggle to Create Content Consistently

Sadly, most business owners aren't consistent with their content posts. It's understandable as you have a lot going on as a business owner, but you need to make posting a habit so that you can continually put yourself out there and be seen. So it comes time to post something and you have nothing ready. At this point is it easier to just not post, or think about what you want to post about, come up with an idea, create the post, get a picture, and then post? It's far easier to skip and that's how most businesses end up randomly posting on their page a few times a month. If you want to be different from the pack, you need to block out time on your calendar for each aspect of the content creation process. During one session, all you're going to do is come up with ideas. Then on your next session, you're going to write the text for those posts. The session after that, you'll get photos ready to go with the posts. Once you've done this, you're now ready to post when the time comes. It doesn't matter what else you have going on because all of the legwork has been done upfront so it's seamless to post at this point.

Cold Outreach Via Email and Phone

Aside from going and talking to people in person, you can reach out via other methods, such as email or over the phone. The thing about an email is that it's easy to ignore and it can be harder to convey your value over the phone rather than in person. You can use cold email and phone calls though to reach more businesses. In your spare time when you're unable to talk to people in person, you can email or call. The people who don't get back to you, you can mark down and go visit them in person when you get the chance. By combining in-person with online outreach, you can increase your chances of gaining a new customer. Here's what you could send as a cold email:

"Hey, my name is Sally and I run my own mobile coffee cart business. First off I really just want to say I appreciate the attention to detail you guys have put into your website. When I worked with a real estate company to buy my home, something that deterred me from a few places when I was looking around were websites that were difficult to navigate and trust. So kudos to you guys! I'm sure being in the real estate world, you understand how important it is to do outreach as a method of gaining new clientele. That's why I'm reaching out to you here today. As part of my services, I bring in a fully stocked cart and serve a full menu of various caffeinated beverages to your employees as they come into work for the day. I'd love to discuss more and do a free test run if you're interested.

Thanks,

Sally"

So in this example, you're outreaching to a real estate office, but it doesn't matter who you're reaching out to, you want to make it personalized. The more specific you can be the better. This will ensure that you're not giving out the same cookie-cutter pitch to everyone. So things will vary from email to email, but that's generally how you want things to flow. Another critical aspect to this email is the fact that you're offering to do a free trial run. You may loathe the idea of doing this, but why should someone trust that you're going to be worth it? This takes the burden of risk off of the customer and puts it on you. Now the potential customer can try out your service risk-free and see how they like it. This will make it far easier to close a sale. One other thing you'll want to do is link to your website at the bottom of the email. This will give the person the chance to learn more about you on their own. Don't assume that they'll try and look you up on their own because that's not going to happen. In most cases, your initial email isn't going to be responded to, and just like with following up for a review, you want to persist and follow up. The smart way to go about this is to reply to the initial email that you sent so that way it appears like a conversation is happening. Here's an example of what to say:

"Hey, I just wanted to follow up regarding the email I sent the other day about my mobile coffee cart. I'd love to set up a time for a free trial run and give out some free coffee to you guys!"

With your follow-up, you want to keep things to the point and hit your main highlight, which is going to be your free trial run. If you're calling over the phone, you can follow a similar script, again though, remember to emphasize a free test run because, without it, it can be harder to get people interested.

Chapter 7: Expanding Your Cart Business Beyond One Cart

With one cart or truck, you can make some good money on the side or even replace your full-time income. You might want to do something more than that though and be a boss. The way that you can do this is by buying another cart and/or truck and having other people handle the fulfillment of the service. Yes, expanding does involve risk, so this could be something you're not interested in doing, which is totally reasonable. However, if you want to maximize your income and truly live life on your own terms where the money is coming in and you're not having to do any of the actual labor, then this information can be of value to you.

Which Comes First the Truck or the Cart

Regardless of how you're operating your business right now, the point will come when you have a decision to make. Do you want to expand by adding in an extra cart or an extra truck? Maybe you want someone to handle the fulfillment so you can focus more of your attention on marketing. Maybe you want someone to handle fulfillment so you can take more of a backseat role in the business. Maybe you want to grow and increase your revenue as much as you can so you'll operate one cart and a second person will operate another. You need to stop and think about how you want to expand and why you want to do it. If your revenue isn't where you'd like for it to be, then it doesn't make sense to hire someone so you can take more of a backseat role in the business. By doing that, you're only increasing your operating expenses without increasing your revenue. More than likely what will make the most sense is to look to have some hired help so that you can be in two places at once. You'll operate a truck or cart and the new person will do the same. As far as a new truck or cart is concerned, I would look to add in an extra cart. The reason being here is that the cart will be cheaper, plain and simple. This means you'll be able to experience more profit sooner.

Where to Find Quality Coffee Baristas?

The idea of having someone else grow your business sounds cool, but where can you go to get quality leads for your position? Job boards are one place that you could look, but the problem is that they do cost money and sure you'll get a lot of applicants, but the majority of them are going to be a waste of your time. You're going to be looking through all of your candidates only to realize that you're only getting a few quality candidates per 100 applicants. Instead of starting with a job board, what you should do instead is go to places where baristas already are. I'm talking about online groups. Online groups are a great way to get your position out there for free and the people who are interested will have a higher chance of being good. You'll of course want to get the group admin's permission to post in the group about your position, but once you get the green light, go ahead and make your post. Post in groups that are local to your area and groups that aren't, but specifically call out the area you live in. You don't want to leave anything to chance. You never know how many people in your area are in a group that includes people across the entire country. If you're not able to find anyone worthy from any online groups, then go ahead and consider looking into a job board. Yes, you will be spending some money, but at least you'll be sure to get some people applying to the job.

Conclusion

Coffee is a great business to be in because people are never going to stop drinking it. So if you're ever looking at your business and you're disappointed in your sales, then just know that it's possible to improve. You're not selling something new that doesn't have an existing market. There's a huge market for coffee, so just continue to refine your sales and marketing skills, and soon enough your business will start to boom. All it takes is a little patience and the willingness to work hard for the life you want!

www.ingramcontent.com/pod-product-compliance
Lightning Source LLC
Chambersburg PA
CBHW070413230526
45471CB00006B/2779